*Profiles of the Presidents*

# WILLIAM JEFFERSON CLINTON

★ ★ ★

*Profiles of the Presidents*

# WILLIAM JEFFERSON
# CLINTON

*by Ann Heinrichs*

Content Adviser: Harry Rubenstein, Curator of Political History Collections, National Museum of American History, Smithsonian Institution

Social Science Adviser: Professor Sherry L. Field, Department of Curriculum and Instruction, College of Education, The University of Texas at Austin

Reading Adviser: Dr. Linda D. Labbo, Department of Reading Education, College of Education, The University of Georgia

COMPASS POINT BOOKS ✦ MINNEAPOLIS, MINNESOTA

Compass Point Books
3722 West 50th Street, #115
Minneapolis, MN 55410

Visit Compass Point Books on the Internet at *www.compasspointbooks.com*
or e-mail your request to *custserv@compasspointbooks.com*

Photographs ©: White House Collection, courtesy White House Historical Association, cover, 3;
David & Peter Turnley/Corbis, 6, 35; AFP/Corbis, 7, 11, 36; AP/Wide World Photos, 9, 10, 16, 24,
25, 34, 54 (top left), 56 (bottom left); Reuters/Jeff Mitchell/Hulton Getty/Archive Photos, 12 (all), 22,
54 (bottom left); Corbis, 13; Hulton Getty/Archive Photos, 15, 19, 43, 55 (all); Bettmann/Corbis, 17,
20, 21, 23; Wally McNamee/Corbis, 26, 27, 30, 31, 32, 46; Reuters/Scott Olson/Hulton Getty/
Archive Photos, 28, 57 (middle left); Reuters/Rick Wilking/Hulton Getty/Archive Photos, 33; Reuters
NewMedia Inc./Corbis, 37, 58 (middle right); Reuters/Win McNamee/Hulton Getty/Archive Photos,
38, 41, 42, 58 (bottom left); Reuters/Hulton Getty/Archive Photos, 39, 40; Reuters/Blake Sell/Hulton
Getty/Archive Photos, 44, 59 (top right); Reuters/Brad Rickerby/Hulton Getty/Archive Photos, 45, 59
(middle left); Reuters/Robert Giroux/Hulton Getty/Archive Photos, 47, 58 (bottom right); Reuters/
Kevin Lamarque/Hulton Getty/Archive Photos, 48; Reuters/Pawel Kopczynski/Hulton Getty/Archive
Photos, 50; PhotoDisc, 56 (top left, bottom right); NASA, 57 (top right); Digital Vision, 59 (bottom
right).

Editors: E. Russell Primm, Emily J. Dolbear, and Melissa McDaniel
Photo Researchers: Svetlana Zhurkina and Jo Miller
Photo Selector: Catherine Neitge
Designer: The Design Lab

Library of Congress Cataloging-in-Publication Data

Heinrichs, Ann.
    William Jefferson Clinton / by Ann Heinrichs.
        p. cm. — (Profiles of the presidents)
    Includes bibliographical references and index.
    Summary: Discusses the life and accomplishments of the Democrat who was elected president to
two successive terms, 1992 and 1996.
    ISBN 0-7565-0207-1 (hardcover)
    1. Clinton, Bill, 1946– —Juvenile literature. 2. Presidents—United States—Biography—Juvenile
literature. [1. Clinton, Bill, 1946– 2. Presidents.]    I. Title. II. Series.
    E886 .H44 2002
    973.929'092—dc21                                                    2001004742

# Table of Contents

★   ★   ★

# The New Democrat

★  ★  ★

At first, people said no one could beat the Republican president of the United States. And certainly not a Democrat. No Democrat had been president for the last twelve years. And certainly not Bill Clinton. He had come

Bill Clinton and ▶
his wife, Hillary

◄ *Bill Clinton was a "New Democrat."*

from a place called Hope, a small town in Arkansas. He wasn't part of the "in crowd" of Washington, D.C. But Clinton proved them wrong.

At age thirty-two, Clinton had been the youngest governor in the United States. In his twelve years as governor of Arkansas, the rest of the country got to know him. He appealed to rich and poor, young and old. People liked his sharp mind, boyish charm, and real concern for people and their problems.

Clinton was the brightest star among the "New Democrats" of the 1990s. The New Democrats believed everyone should have a chance to succeed in the United States. But they also said that people should take responsibility for themselves and be involved in the world around them. As a New Democrat, Clinton talked about things that average people cared about—jobs, education, crime, and the economy.

At a time when millions were struggling to make ends meet, Clinton promised a brighter tomorrow. It was just what Americans wanted to hear, and they elected him twice. Many got what they wanted. When Clinton was president, America enjoyed the longest period of peace and economic prosperity in its history.

Elected at age forty-six, Bill Clinton was one of the youngest presidents in U.S. history. In time, he became the second president ever to be **impeached,** or charged with serious crimes, by the House of Representatives. Yet, even then, a record-breaking number of Americans approved of the way Clinton was doing his job.

Early in his career, Clinton was disappointed when he lost an election. When he won the next time around, people called him the "Comeback Kid." He made a comment then to explain what kept him going: "The main thing is never quit, never quit, never quit." He never did.

Bill Clinton hugged his mother, Virginia Kelley, during inauguration festivities in 1993.

# The Early Years

★  ★  ★

Hope is a small town in the piney woods of southwest Arkansas. Only about 7,000 people lived there when Virginia Cassidy married Bill Blythe. Virginia was a young nurse, and Bill was a heavy-equipment salesman. Soon they were expecting their first baby.

Hoping to find a better job, Bill traveled to Chicago, Illinois. While he was driving back to Arkansas, one of the tires on his car blew out. His car rolled over and landed near a drainage ditch. Bill drowned trying to make his way back to the highway for help. Three months before her baby was due, Virginia found herself alone, without a husband.

William Jefferson Blythe died three months before his son was born.

On August 19, 1946, Virginia welcomed her new baby boy. She named him William Jefferson Blythe IV, after his father. Everyone called him Billy. Because she had to support her baby son by herself, Virginia decided to take higher-level nursing classes. She had to go to New Orleans, Louisiana, for her studies. Meanwhile, Billy stayed in Hope with Virginia's parents, Edith and Eldridge Cassidy. They owned a grocery store in a poor section of Hope.

▲ *Bill Clinton's boyhood home in Hope*

By the time he was four, Billy could read and count. When Virginia returned from New Orleans, she sent him to Miss Marie Purkins' School for Little Folks. Classmates remember that he loved to wear his cowboy boots. Soon after, Virginia married a car salesman

*Bill Clinton in 1951* ▲

*Bill Clinton, left,* ▶
*with his mother,*
*Virginia, and his*
*half-brother, Roger,*
*in 1959*

named Roger
Clinton. The family
then moved to Hot
Springs, Arkansas.
Since the 1800s, this
town had drawn
tourists. They came
for its healthful
mineral waters.

In Hot Springs,
Billy decided on his
own to join the local
Baptist Church. With
Bible in hand, he
walked alone to
church and back on
Sundays. When he
was ten, a new

baby—Roger Jr.—joined the family. In high school, Billy
changed his own last name to Clinton.

At Hot Springs High School, Billy got an early start in
politics by running for school offices. "You could tell this
boy was going places," one of his classmates said. But most

*Bill Clinton, shown in this 1992 photo, started playing the saxophone in school.*

of all, Billy loved music. He played saxophone in the school band, and he loved hearing the gospel music at church.

Life at home, however, was not always pleasant. Billy's stepfather drank heavily and had a bad temper. Sometimes he took out his anger on Virginia and the children. Once he even fired a gun into the wall. Billy often found himself trying to make peace between his mother and stepfather. By the time he was fourteen, Billy was old enough to fight back. He threatened his stepfather, telling him never to lay a hand on his mother again. In time, the couple divorced.

Billy thought of becoming a professional musician or a doctor. But all that changed when he was chosen for the American Legion Boys Nation program. With boys from around the country, he traveled to Washington, D.C., to learn about government and leadership. While he was there, he met President John F. Kennedy. Young Billy shook hands with the president in the White House Rose Garden. It was an experience the teenager would never forget. By the time he got back to Arkansas, he had made up his mind: Politics was the life for him.

As a teen, Bill Clinton shook hands with President John F. Kennedy during a 1963 visit to the White House.

# Off to Washington

★ ★ ★

The nation's capital was the place Bill Clinton wanted to be. So in 1964, he entered Georgetown University in Washington, D.C. There he studied international affairs.

A 1966 ▶
Georgetown
University photo
shows Bill
Clinton, left, with
two fellow
students.

Georgetown was an expensive school, but Bill managed with the help of **scholarships** and part-time jobs.

Bill was a bit of an outsider at Georgetown. It was a Catholic university and he was a Baptist. He was from small-town Arkansas; the university was in the big city of Washington. But Bill put

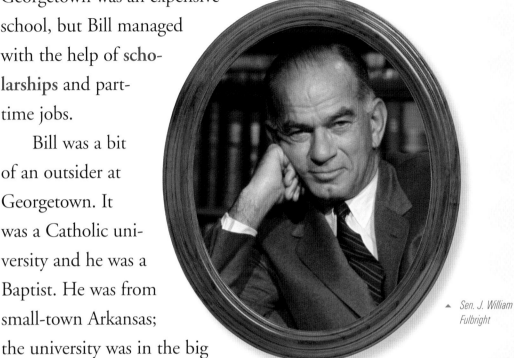

▲ *Sen. J. William Fulbright*

his energy and charm to work. His fellow students elected him president of both his freshman and sophomore classes.

In his senior year, Bill worked as a **clerk** for the powerful Foreign Relations Committee in the U.S. Senate. Its chairman was Senator J. William Fulbright of Arkansas. Bill was proud to see an Arkansan in such an important job. He came to have a deep respect for Fulbright.

At that time, the United States was fighting a war in Southeast Asia. Fulbright did not believe the United States should be involved in the Vietnam War. Working in the Senate, Bill talked to many other important politicians about the war. He, too, began to object to America's participation in the war.

Just before he graduated in 1968, Bill received good news. He had won a Rhodes scholarship to study at Oxford University in England for two years. While he was there, however, he received a **draft** notice calling him to military duty. This raised some difficult questions for Bill.

On the one hand, he was against the war. On the other hand, he had grown up in the South, where people considered military service an honor and a duty. Bill made his decision. To put off being drafted, he joined the Army Reserve Officers Training Corps (ROTC) at the University of Arkansas. Later he withdrew from the ROTC. His avoidance of military service would come up when he ran for president.

Back in England, he again put his name in for the draft. At that time in the United States, young men who might be drafted were given numbers at random. Starting with number 1, people were called to duty in numerical order. Bill received such a high number—311—that he was never called.

▲ *Oxford University
in 1968*

In 1970, Bill entered Yale University Law School in
New Haven, Connecticut. There he met a bright young
law student named Hillary Rodham. The two found they
had a lot in common. In 1972, Democrat George

Sen. George McGovern gives the victory sign during his 1972 run for the presidency.

McGovern was running for president against the incumbent, Republican Richard Nixon. Both Bill and Hillary worked for McGovern, with Bill managing his **campaign** in Texas. Nixon, however, won the election.

# Arkansas Politics

★ ★ ★

After law school, Clinton moved back to Arkansas. Both he and Hillary taught at the University of Arkansas Law School in Fayetteville. Clinton soon saw a chance to enter

◀ President Richard Nixon, left, and Vice President Spiro Agnew in 1972

politics. Republican congressman John Paul Hammerschmidt was running for reelection in 1974. Hammerschmidt supported President Nixon, and Nixon was

becoming less popular.
Clinton decided to run against
Hammerschmidt. Clinton lost,
but only by a narrow margin.
As a result, people began to
notice the young Democrat.

Clinton and Hillary got
married in 1975. A year later,
he ran for Arkansas attorney
general. This time, he won. In
1978, he reached even higher,
winning the race for governor
of Arkansas. At age thirty-two,
Clinton was the youngest governor in the country. Their

▲ *Bill and Hillary
Clinton with baby
Chelsea in 1980*

heads spinning from rising so fast, the Clintons moved into
the governor's mansion in Little Rock, the state capital. In
February 1980, their daughter, Chelsea, was born.

Clinton's lack of experience in politics worked against
him. He brought in advisers from out of state to help

★

improve schools and the environment. He later believed
that he had tried to do too much in too short a time. To
improve the state's roads, he raised gasoline taxes. This was
an unpopular move. Clinton was also blamed for the way
he handled a crisis at Fort Chaffe in the town of Fort
Smith. The U.S. government had placed 18,000 refugees
there. They had come from the island nation of Cuba,
which lies off the coast of Florida. A riot broke out in the
camp, and several buildings were burned. In 1980, voters

*▲ Bill Clinton chatted with fellow governors Pierre du Pont and Robert Ray in 1979.*

Bill and Hillary Clinton celebrate his 1982 primary election victory. The "Comeback Kid" went on to win back the governorship of Arkansas that year.

elected Republican Frank White as governor.

After his defeat, Clinton began to plan his next campaign for governor. He knew he had to be more careful. When he won the 1982 election, people called him the "Comeback Kid." Clinton served as governor of Arkansas for the next ten years.

This time, Clinton handled his job differently. He learned to set realistic goals and to operate on a small budget. He also learned to get along with the **legislature,** which was controlled by Republicans. This was good practice for the years ahead.

As governor, Clinton hoped to improve the low status of Arkansas among the other states. Arkansas ranked last—or

near last—in economic conditions, income, and education.

Clinton's changes in the state's education system were his greatest achievement. One new policy—compulsory testing for all teachers—caught national attention. Other policies lowered dropout rates, raised teachers' wages, and improved college-entrance test scores. Clinton also reformed the state's welfare system. New programs got more people off welfare and into the workforce. And he appointed more women and minorities to government posts than had ever served in Arkansas before.

▲ *Bill Clinton, top right, met with President George Bush and other dignitaries during an education meeting in 1989. Education reform was important to Clinton.*

# A New Generation

★ ★ ★

All this time, Clinton had his eye on a prize—the presidency. Calling himself a "New Democrat," he worked on reshaping what Democrats stood for. In 1990, he became chairman of the Democratic Leadership Council. These New Democrats believed that everyone should have a

President Bill ▶ Clinton spoke to the Democratic Leadership Council in 1993. He served as the group's chairman when he was governor of Arkansas.

chance to succeed. In return, people had to take responsibility and do their part. The New Democrats hoped that the country's many different groups would work together.

In 1991, Clinton declared that he was running for president in 1992. During the campaign, issues came up about his personal life and his avoidance of the draft. Still Clinton was chosen as the Democratic candidate. He would run against President George H.W. Bush, a Republican, and Ross Perot, an independent.

Clinton chose Tennessee senator Albert A. Gore Jr. as his vice presidential **running mate.** They believed the economy was the major issue of the race. A campaign adviser

▲ *Bill Clinton debated President George Bush, left, and Ross Perot on TV during the 1992 presidential campaign*

put it this way: "It's the economy, stupid!"

Clinton and Gore brought their campaign to the people, taking bus trips from town to town. Clinton stopped at coffee shops, shopping malls, and town squares all around the country. Along the bus routes, crowds cheered and waited hours to see him. When his aides were worn out, Clinton only seemed to get more energy. He loved getting close to people, shaking their hands, and asking about their problems.

Clinton knew people were suffering from hard times. He talked about jobs, health care, crime, and other issues important to the average person. He wanted people to

*Bill and Hillary ▶ Clinton, left, and Al and Tipper Gore wave to the crowd during a campaign rally in 1992.*

believe they could have a better life and fulfill their dreams. Referring to his birthplace, he said, "I still believe in a place called Hope."

Voters must have believed, too. On November 3, 1992, they elected him the forty-second president of the United States. At age forty-six, he was one of the youngest presidents in U.S. history. After ten years in the governor's mansion, the Clintons packed up to move into the White House.

President Clinton and Vice President Gore were part of a new **generation** in American politics. Clinton was the first U.S. president born after World War II (1939–1945). On January 20, 1993, in his first speech as president, he called on Americans to seize their moment in history. "Today, a new generation . . . assumes new responsibilities," he said. "This is our time. Let us embrace it!"

Now, for the first time in twelve years, both the president and a majority of the members of Congress were Democrats. This was a great chance for Clinton to carry out his plans. In his first week in office, he appointed the First Lady to head a task force to improve the health-care system in the United States.

Millions of Americans had no health insurance at all. The task force was organized to find ways to make health

*Vice President ▶
Al Gore and
President Bill
Clinton*

care available to all. It wouldn't be easy. Two presidents—Franklin D. Roosevelt and Lyndon Johnson—had tried and failed to make major changes in the health-care system. But Clinton believed it was time to make it work. The task force worked long and hard and presented its suggestions. However, Congress could not agree on how to make reforms. Once again, the health-care issue died.

▲ *Hillary Clinton headed a task force to study health care reform.*

The Democrats' control of Congress lasted only two

years. In the 1994 elections, Republicans won more seats in both the Senate and the House of Representatives. For the first time in forty years, Republicans controlled both houses of Congress. The Republicans were excited. They were sure a Republican could take the presidency back in 1996. Newt Gingrich, the Speaker of the House of Representatives, led the most **conservative** group in the Republican Party. They sometimes seemed to be out to destroy Clinton and his policies. After Clinton's attempts at fixing the health-care system failed, he turned to other issues. He pushed for laws to improve education and to help working parents care for sick children. He supported stricter laws to protect the environment and control the sale of handguns. Clinton, with Republican support, also changed the welfare system with a plan to get people back to work. Through his national service plan, students could do public service in exchange for a college education.

*Newt Gingrich* ▲

◄ *President Clinton explained how his budget plan would reduce the deficit.*

Clinton's main goal was getting the economy back on its feet. He started by trying to balance the nation's budget. The government was operating at a huge **deficit**—it was spending much more money than it was taking in. When Clinton took office, the deficit was $290 billion—the largest deficit in American history. Clinton made a budget for 1996 that cut the deficit greatly. It cut spending and raised taxes on the wealthiest Americans.

Republicans opposed Clinton's plan. They wanted to lower the deficit by cutting money spent on welfare,

GOP's Certified
Balanced Budget

President Clinton's
Washington Gimmick

*House Speaker
Newt Gingrich,
left, and Senate
Majority Leader
Bob Dole were
opposed to
President Clinton's
budget plan.*

education, and the environment. To force Clinton to give
in, Republicans kept resisting him until the 1995 budget
ran out. This meant there was no more money to spend for
the rest of the year. The Federal government was forced to
shut down. Clinton still refused to give in. It worked. The
Republicans gave in and approved his budget. Most
Americans were on Clinton's side. After the budget battle,
the Republicans realized it might not be so easy to win
back the presidency.

The new budget had a big effect on the country.

Interest rates—the amount people have to pay to borrow money—dropped. As a result, more Americans than ever could afford to buy a house. Companies were able to build and expand, creating millions of new jobs. The percentage of people without jobs fell to its lowest point in decades. The country entered its longest period of economic growth since the early 1960s.

*President Clinton spoke during a ceremony in Paris in 1995 to mark the signing of a peace agreement that ended the fighting in Bosnia.*

In foreign affairs, Clinton showed a talent for settling differences peacefully. One after another, hot spots around the world were flaring up. Clinton stepped in to help make peace in Northern Ireland. Government leaders in both Great Britain and Ireland asked Clinton to make phone calls at important times in the peace process. He also brought Israel and Jordan together to sign a peace treaty. In November 1995, he brought about the Dayton Accords,

*Hillary Clinton has worked hard for many years on children's issues.*

ending nearly four years of bitter war in Bosnia.

The First Lady played a role in foreign affairs, too. She toured Latin America to promote goodwill. Then Chelsea joined her on a trip through South Asia. Chelsea sometimes asked more questions than the reporters did. In China, Hillary made headlines when she gave a speech at an international conference on women's rights.

Hillary was also making speaking tours for her own causes. For many years, she had worked for children's issues. In 1996, she published a book

called *It Takes a Village.*
The title was based on the
African saying, "It takes a
village to raise a child."
The whole society works
together, she said, to give
children what they need to
grow and succeed.

At the same time, some
members of Congress were
busy looking into Clinton's
past. They charged that he and Hillary had made money
on an illegal land deal in Arkansas in the 1980s. They
called for an **investigation,** and Clinton himself agreed. In
1994, Attorney General Janet Reno appointed someone to
investigate the so-called Whitewater affair. The Clintons
were later found innocent. But as the investigation grew
and changed focus over time, it led to the biggest **crisis** in
Clinton's presidency.

▲ *Attorney General
Janet Reno*

In 1996, Democrats again chose Clinton to run for
president. A short time later, the Clintons were saying
good-bye to Chelsea. She would be a freshman at Stanford
University in California in September 1997.

*Chelsea, Hillary and Bill Clinton campaign in 1996.*

Clinton faced Republican Robert Dole in the election. By this time, Clinton's rivals were accusing him of serious wrongdoing. But most Americans were enjoying the best economic time of their lives. On Election Day, November 5, 1996, Clinton won a second term. He became the first Democratic president to be elected to two terms since Franklin Delano Roosevelt in the 1940s.

# The Second Time Around

★ ★ ★

"**P**resident Truman said if you want a friend in Washington, you need to get a dog."

Clinton was joking with reporters as he played with his new puppy on the White House lawn. The Clintons had just adopted a chocolate Labrador retriever. Clinton's favorite uncle had died in June, so he named the dog Buddy in his memory. Now the Clintons were trying to make peace between Buddy and Socks, the

▲ Bill Clinton with his puppy, Buddy

39

Socks walks on ▶ the desk of presidential secretary Betty Currie.

Socks Clinton
Chief Executive Cat

family cat. As Clinton said, "It's kind of like peace in Northern Ireland or the Middle East."

Clinton's second term would be much rougher than the first term, but his economic policies were working. He was proud to announce that, for the first time in nearly thirty years, the government was spending less money than it was taking in.

Foreign affairs still took up much of Clinton's time. He had recently named a new secretary of state, Madeleine Albright. She would play an important part in peace talks in the Middle East. In March 1998, Clinton and Hillary began a trip to six African nations. It was the first time a

◄ Madeleine Albright, flanked by Al Gore and Bill Clinton, became the highest ranking woman in government history when she became secretary of state in 1997.

U.S. president had visited **sub-Saharan** Africa in more than twenty years. A month later, warring sides in Northern Ireland agreed to a peace settlement. Clinton was happy to know his peace efforts were working.

A tearful President Clinton asked for forgiveness during a national prayer breakfast at the White House in 1998.

Meanwhile, the Whitewater investigation had started looking into Clinton's personal life. He was accused of having had improper relations with a young female White House **intern.** When he was questioned about it, Clinton did not tell the truth. In December 1998, the House of Representatives voted to impeach Clinton, or charge him with crimes. By law, the next step was a trial in the Senate.

Only one president in U.S. history had been

impeached before. President
Andrew Johnson was
impeached in 1868 because
his enemies felt he was
too easy on the South
after the Civil War. In
President Johnson's trial,
the Senate found him
not guilty by just one
vote. In the 1970s, the
House had come close to
impeaching President Nixon
over the Watergate affair. To keep
from being impeached, Nixon resigned his office.

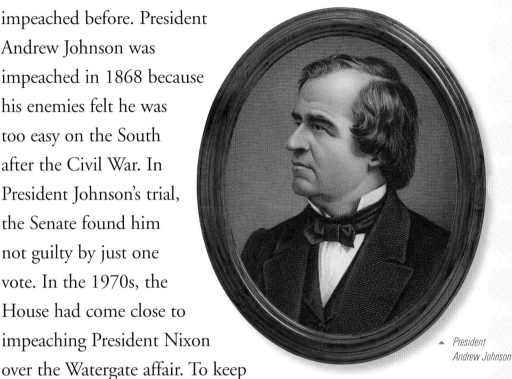

▲ *President
Andrew Johnson*

While the House of Representatives was building its
case against Clinton, many voters were choosing new
congressmen. In the 1998 elections, several Republicans
lost their seats in the House of Representatives. Newt
Gingrich, the leading Republican in the House, quit a
few days later. In January 1999, more Americans than
ever liked the way Clinton was doing his job. It seemed
they cared more about the booming economy than about
Clinton's personal life.

▲ *President Clinton apologized to the country for his mistakes after he was found not guilty by the U.S. Senate.*

In February 1999, the Senate voted that Clinton was not guilty, and he told the nation he was sorry for the mistakes he had made. In September 2000, the six-year Whitewater investigation finally came to an end. Millions of dollars had been spent on it. The Clintons were cleared of any wrongdoing.

Meanwhile, the First Lady had been moving ahead

with plans of her own. Hillary Clinton was one of the most popular First Ladies ever. Like her husband, she was devoted to public service. She turned this into action by running for U.S. senator from New York. When the Democrats chose her to run, President Clinton stood by and watched proudly, just as she had always stood by him. In her speech, she thanked him for his support. She said, "I could not be

▲ *Hillary Clinton shook hands with supporters as she ran for a U.S. Senate seat from New York in 2000.*

▲ *Bill Clinton and Al Gore congratulate the new president, George W. Bush, left.*

prouder as an American and as a New Yorker to have a president who has meant so much to our country." When Hillary won in the fall, she became the only First Lady ever elected to public office.

Vice President Al Gore was not so lucky in his own campaign. Clinton would be stepping down, and Gore hoped to take his place in the White House. He ran against George W. Bush, son of the president Clinton had beaten eight years before. The race was so close that it took weeks to settle who had won. More people had voted for Gore. But Bush received more votes from the **electoral college**, so he was elected president.

# Grateful to Serve

★ ★ ★

"I love my job. I'm grateful for the opportunity to serve." President Clinton often expressed this feeling, even when times were tough.

As president, Clinton served by bringing hope and good fortune to the nation. Thanks to his economic policies, more people were able to buy their own homes than at any other time in U.S.

◄ The country's bank account improved while Bill Clinton was president.

history. With 22 million new jobs, the percentage of unemployed people was at its lowest level in thirty years. Millions of people moved from welfare to work, and crime dropped

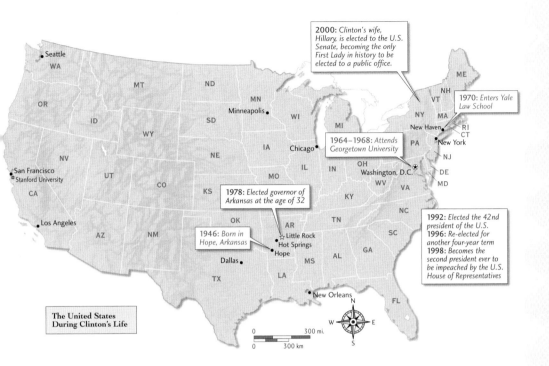

2000: Clinton's wife, Hillary, is elected to the U.S. Senate, becoming the only First Lady in history to be elected to a public office.

1970: Enters Yale Law School

1964–1968: Attends Georgetown University

1978: Elected governor of Arkansas at the age of 32

1992: Elected the 42nd president of the U.S.
1996: Re-elected for another four-year term
1998: Becomes the second president ever to be impeached by the U.S. House of Representatives

1946: Born in Hope, Arkansas

The United States During Clinton's Life

to a twenty-six-year low. Clinton also made the nation's air, drinking water, and food safer and helped preserve more of our forests. Meanwhile, the nation's bank account was in much better shape.

Few presidents have suffered more public attacks than Clinton did. Yet no president gave the nation a longer period of economic good times.

Clinton once said, "The main thing is never quit, never quit, never quit." He never did. And his desire to serve the nation will probably continue for many years to come. In his farewell address to the nation, Clinton said:

"I am profoundly grateful to you for twice giving me the honor to serve. . . . My days in this office are nearly through, but my days of service, I hope, are not."

*Former President Clinton looked at earthquake damage in India in 2001. He was on a trip to raise money for earthquake victims.*

# GLOSSARY

★ ★ ★

**campaign**—a series of efforts to win an election

**clerk**—office worker

**conservative**—believing in small government and old-fashioned values

**crisis**—a time of danger

**deficit**—the loss created when government spends more than it takes in

**draft**—a system of selecting people for military service

**electoral college**—a group of people who elect the U.S. president. Each state is given a certain number of electoral votes; the candidate who receives the most votes from the people is awarded the state's electoral votes.

**generation**—a group of people born in the same time period

**impeach**—to charge a public official with a serious crime

**intern**—a person working for little or no money to gain experience

**investigation**—an official examination

**legislature**—the part of government that makes or changes laws

**running mate**—person running for public office on another person's ticket

**scholarships**—money given to students for their education

**sub-Saharan**—the part of Africa south of the Sahara Desert

# WILLIAM JEFFERSON CLINTON'S LIFE AT A GLANCE

★ ★ ★

## PERSONAL

| | |
|---|---|
| Nickname: | Bill; Comeback Kid |
| Born: | August 19, 1946 |
| Birthplace: | Hope, Arkansas |
| Father's name: | William Jefferson Blythe III |
| Stepfather: | Roger Clinton |
| Mother's name: | Virginia Divine Cassidy Blythe Clinton Kelley |
| Education: | Graduated from Georgetown University in 1968, attended Oxford University from 1968 to 1970, graduated from Yale University Law School in 1973 |
| Wife's name: | Hillary Rodham Clinton |
| Married: | October 11, 1975 |
| Children: | Chelsea Victoria Clinton (1980– ) |

## PUBLIC

| | |
|---|---|
| Occupation before presidency: | Lawyer, public official |
| Military service: | None |
| Other government positions: | Arkansas attorney general, 1976–1978; governor of Arkansas, 1978–1980 and 1982–1992 |
| Political party: | Democrat |
| Vice President: | Albert Gore Jr. (1993–2001) |
| Dates in office: | January 20, 1993– January 20, 2001 |
| Presidential opponents: | President George H. W. Bush (Republican) and H. Ross Perot (independent), 1992; Senator Robert Dole (Republican) and H. Ross Perot (Reform Party), 1996 |
| Number of votes (Electoral College): | 44,908,233 of 104,405,155 (370 of 538), 1992; 47,402,357 of 96,456,345 (379 of 538), 1996 |
| Writings: | *Putting People First: How We Can All Change America* (1992), coauthored with Albert Gore Jr. |

★

**William Jefferson Clinton's Cabinet**

*Secretary of state:*
Warren M. Christopher (1993–1997)
Madeleine Albright (1997–2001)

*Secretary of the treasury:*
Lloyd M. Bentsen (1993–1994)
Robert E. Rubin (1995–1999)
Lawrence H. Summers (1999–2001)

*Secretary of defense:*
Les Aspin Jr. (1993–1994)
William J. Perry (1994–1997)
William Cohen (1997–2001)

*Attorney general:*
Janet Reno (1993–2001)

*Secretary of the interior:*
Bruce Babbitt (1993–2001)

*Secretary of agriculture:*
Mike Espy (1993–1994)
Dan Glickman (1994–2001)

*Secretary of commerce:*
Ronald H. Brown (1993–1996)
Mickey Kantor (1996–1997)
William Daley (1997–2000)
Norman Y. Mineta (2000–2001)

*Secretary of labor:*
Robert B. Reich (1993–1997)
Alexis M. Herman (1997–2001)

*Secretary of health and human services:*
Donna E. Shalala (1993–2001)

*Secretary of housing and urban development:*
Henry G. Cisneros (1993–1997)
Andrew M. Cuomo (1997–2001)

*Secretary of transportation:*
Federico F. Peña (1993–1997)
Rodney Slater (1997–2001)

*Secretary of energy:*
Hazel R. O'Leary (1993–1997)
Federico F. Peña (1997–1998)
Bill Richardson (1998–2001)

*Secretary of education:*
Richard W. Riley (1993–2001)

*Secretary of veterans affairs:*
Jesse Brown (1993–1997)
Togo D. West Jr. (1998–2000)
Hershel W. Gober (2000–2001)

# WILLIAM JEFFERSON CLINTON'S LIFE AND TIMES

★ ★ ★

## CLINTON'S LIFE

August 19, 1946
Clinton is born
in Hope,
Arkansas, to
Virginia
Blythe three
months after
his father, Bill
Blythe (left), is
killed in a car crash

Mother marries Roger 1951
Clinton; half-brother
Roger Jr. born in 1956

**1950**

## WORLD EVENTS

1945 America bombs the
Japanese cities of
Hiroshima and
Nagasaki using
atomic bombs

The United Nations
is founded

1949 Birth of the People's
Republic of China

1953 The first Europeans
climb Mount Everest

1955 Disneyland, the first
theme park in the
United States, opens
in Anaheim,
California

1959 The Barbie doll
debuts

Fidel Castro becomes
prime minister of
Cuba

## CLINTON'S LIFE

As part of the American Legion Boys Nation program, shakes hands with President John F. Kennedy (above) — 1963

Wins Rhodes scholarship to study at Oxford University (below) — 1968

Graduates from law school and returns to Arkansas to teach law — 1973

**1960**

**1970**

## WORLD EVENTS

1961    Yuri Gagarin is the first human to enter space

1962    Rachel Carson's influential book *Silent Spring* is published, increasing environmental awareness nationwide

1964    G.I. Joe makes his debut as the first boy's "action figure"

1967    The first heart transplant is attempted

1968    Civil rights leader Martin Luther King Jr. is assassinated

1969    U.S. astronauts are the first humans to land on the Moon

1971    Gloria Steinem founds *Ms.* magazine, part of the women's liberation movement of the time

       The first microprocessor is produced by Intel

1973    Arab oil embargo creates concerns about natural resources

## CLINTON'S LIFE

Is elected attorney general of Arkansas · 1976

Is elected governor of Arkansas · 1978

Loses the governor's race in his biggest political defeat · 1980

Is reelected governor of Arkansas (below) · 1982

## WORLD EVENTS

1973 · Spanish artist Pablo Picasso dies

1974 · Scientists find that chlorofluorocarbons —chemicals in coolants and propellants —are damaging to the Earth's ozone layer

1976 · U.S. military academies admit women

1978 · The first test-tube baby conceived outside its mother's womb is born in Oldham, England

**1980**

1982 · Maya Lin designs the Vietnam War Memorial (below), commemorating the Americans who died

1983 · The AIDS (acquired immune deficiency syndrome) virus is identified

## CLINTON'S LIFE

Serves as chairman    1986–
of the National       1987
Governor's
Association

January 20, takes    1993
oath of office as
42nd president of the
United States

In October, plan to
change health-care
system fails

## WORLD EVENTS

1986    The U.S. space
        shuttle *Challenger*
        explodes, killing all
        seven on board

**1990**

1990    Political prisoner
        Nelson Mandela,
        a leader of the anti-
        apartheid movement
        in South Africa, is
        released. Mandela
        becomes president of
        South Africa in 1994

1991    The Soviet Union
        collapses and is
        replaced by the
        Commonwealth of
        Independent States

        Conflict between Iraq
        and Kuwait in the
        Persian Gulf begins

| Presidential Election Results: | | Popular Votes | Electoral Votes |
| --- | --- | --- | --- |
| 1992 | William Jefferson Clinton | 44,909,889 | 370 |
| | George H. W. Bush | 39,104,545 | 168 |
| 1996 | William Jefferson Clinton | 45,628,667 | 379 |
| | Robert Dole | 37,869,435 | 159 |

| CLINTON'S LIFE | | WORLD EVENTS |
|---|---|---|
| In November, North American Free Trade Agreement (NAFTA) creates a free trade zone among Canada, Mexico, and the United States | 1993 | |
| In September, helps Jean-Bertrand Aristide regain control of Haiti | 1994 | Genocide of 500,000 to 1 million of the minority Tutsi group by rival Hutu people in Rwanda |
| In December, General Agreement on Tariffs and Trade (GATT) is expanded, reducing trade barriers | | |
| Wins reelection, becoming the first Democratic president to be elected twice since Franklin Delano Roosevelt | 1996 | 1996 · A sheep is cloned in Scotland |
| Changes in welfare system approved by Congress | | |
| Names Madeleine Albright the first female secretary of state (above) | | |
| The national budget shows a $70-billion surplus | 1998 | |
| December 19, is impeached | | |

## CLINTON'S LIFE

## WORLD EVENTS

From January 7 to February 6, is tried in the Senate; he is found not guilty

In March, air strikes launched against Yugoslavia to stop attacks on Kosovo

Helps work out the Wye Agreements, which give the Palestinians some power in the Gaza Strip and West Bank

Plays an important role in bringing peace to the Balkans

1999

Hillary Clinton is elected a U.S. senator from New York

2000

**2000**

2000

Draft of the human genome is completed

Violent protests in Seattle against the International Monetary Fund and World Bank draw attention to resistance against these organizations

In January, retires from the presidency and moves to Chappaqua, New York

2001

2001

Terrorist attacks on the two World Trade Center towers in New York City and on the Pentagon in Washington, D.C., leave thousands dead

# UNDERSTANDING WILLIAM JEFFERSON CLINTON AND HIS PRESIDENCY

★ ★ ★

## IN THE LIBRARY

Cwiklik, Robert. *Bill Clinton: President of the 90s.*
Brookfield, Conn.: Copper Beech Books, 1997.

Kelly, Michael. *Bill Clinton.* New York: Chelsea House, 1998.

Landau, Elaine. *Bill Clinton and His Presidency.*
Danbury, Conn.: Franklin Watts, 1997.

Levert, Suzanne. *Hillary Rodham Clinton: First Lady.*
Brookfield, Conn.: Millbrook Press, 1994.

Schuman, Michael A. *Bill Clinton.* Springfield, N.J.:
Enslow Publishers, 1999.

## ON THE WEB

**Internet Public Library: William Jefferson Clinton**
*http://www.potus.com/wjclinton.html*
For information about William Jefferson Clinton, including  links
to biographies, copies of his inaugural addresses, and more

### Time.com – Clinton's Last Days
*http://www.time.com/time/photoessays/clintonlastdays/*
For a photo-essay of Bill Clinton's last days in office

### The American President
*http://www.americanpresident.org/KoTrain/Courses/BC/BC_In_Brief.htm*
For a biography of Bill Clinton, including quotations and a photo gallery

## CLINTON HISTORIC SITES ACROSS THE COUNTRY

**The Clinton Birthplace Foundation, Inc.**
P.O. Box 1925
Hope, Arkansas 71802-1925
870/777-4455
To call or write the Clinton Birthplace Foundation for information on visiting Bill Clinton's first home

**Arkansas Governor's Mansion**
1800 Center Street
Little Rock, Arkansas 72206
*http://www.accessarkansas.org/governor/mansion/index.html*
To see the home of the Clinton family during Bill Clinton's years as governor of Arkansas

**Hot Springs Convention and Visitors Bureau**
134 Convention Boulevard
Hot Springs National Park, Arkansas 71902
501/321-2277
To see the houses, schools, and churches where Bill Clinton spent his youth

# THE U.S. PRESIDENTS
## (Years in Office)

★　★　★

1. **George Washington**
(March 4, 1789-March 3, 1797)

2. **John Adams**
(March 4, 1797-March 3, 1801)

3. **Thomas Jefferson**
(March 4, 1801-March 3, 1809)

4. **James Madison**
(March 4, 1809-March 3, 1817)

5. **James Monroe**
(March 4, 1817-March 3, 1825)

6. **John Quincy Adams**
(March 4, 1825-March 3, 1829)

7. **Andrew Jackson**
(March 4, 1829-March 3, 1837)

8. **Martin Van Buren**
(March 4, 1837-March 3, 1841)

9. **William Henry Harrison**
(March 6, 1841-April 4, 1841)

10. **John Tyler**
(April 6, 1841-March 3, 1845)

11. **James K. Polk**
(March 4, 1845-March 3, 1849)

12. **Zachary Taylor**
(March 5, 1849-July 9, 1850)

13. **Millard Fillmore**
(July 10, 1850-March 3, 1853)

14. **Franklin Pierce**
(March 4, 1853-March 3, 1857)

15. **James Buchanan**
(March 4, 1857-March 3, 1861)

16. **Abraham Lincoln**
(March 4, 1861-April 15, 1865)

17. **Andrew Johnson**
(April 15, 1865-March 3, 1869)

18. **Ulysses S. Grant**
(March 4, 1869-March 3, 1877)

19. **Rutherford B. Hayes**
(March 4, 1877-March 3, 1881)

20. **James Garfield**
(March 4, 1881-Sept 19, 1881)

21. **Chester Arthur**
(Sept 20, 1881-March 3, 1885)

22. **Grover Cleveland**
(March 4, 1885-March 3, 1889)

23. **Benjamin Harrison**
(March 4, 1889-March 3, 1893)

24. **Grover Cleveland**
(March 4, 1893-March 3, 1897)

25. **William McKinley**
(March 4, 1897–
September 14, 1901)

26. **Theodore Roosevelt**
(September 14, 1901–
March 3, 1909)

27. **William Howard Taft**
(March 4, 1909-March 3, 1913)

28. **Woodrow Wilson**
(March 4, 1913-March 3, 1921)

29. **Warren G. Harding**
(March 4, 1921-August 2, 1923)

30. **Calvin Coolidge**
(August 3, 1923-March 3, 1929)

31. **Herbert Hoover**
(March 4, 1929-March 3, 1933)

32. **Franklin D. Roosevelt**
(March 4, 1933-April 12, 1945)

33. **Harry S. Truman**
(April 12, 1945–
January 20, 1953)

34. **Dwight D. Eisenhower**
(January 20, 1953–
January 20, 1961)

35. **John F. Kennedy**
(January 20, 1961–
November 22, 1963)

36. **Lyndon B. Johnson**
(November 22, 1963–
January 20, 1969)

37. **Richard M. Nixon**
(January 20, 1969–
August 9, 1974)

38. **Gerald R. Ford**
(August 9, 1974–
January 20, 1977)

39. **James Earl Carter**
(January 20, 1977–
January 20, 1981)

40. **Ronald Reagan**
(January 20, 1981–
January 20, 1989)

41. **George H. W. Bush**
(January 20, 1989–
January 20, 1993)

42. William Jefferson Clinton
(January 20, 1993–
January 20, 2001)

43. **George W. Bush**
(January 20, 2001- )

# INDEX

★ ★ ★

## ABOUT THE AUTHOR

Ann Heinrichs grew up in Fort Smith, Arkansas. She began playing the piano at age three and thought she would grow up to be a pianist. Instead, she became a writer. Now she has written more than fifty books for children and young adults. Several of her books have won national awards. Ms. Heinrichs now lives in Chicago, Illinois. She enjoys martial arts and traveling to faraway countries.